Mommy Time-Out
Means Mommy Can...

by Colleen Phillips and Feli Robles   photographs by Kelley Hernandez

Mommy Time-Out Means Mommy Can... ™
by Colleen Phillips and Feli Robles
Photographs by Kelley Hernandez

Published by 3 Feet From Gold, LLC / Mommy Time-Out (www.mommytimeout.com)

ISBN 978-0-989-0540-0-3

Printed in the U.S.A.

Table of Contents

For all overwhelmed mothers.

Please, take time for yourselves.

Introduction

This photo-driven book encourages mothers to take a "Mommy Time-Out" and do something for themselves – a bubble bath, lunch with friends, or simply watching their favorite TV show without interruption.

As moms ourselves, we know that mothers tend to feel guilty at the thought of spending time or money on themselves. Some have the benefit of assistance and support from family and friends, some do not.

Regardless of the "mother type," it is our goal that this book, as well as the growing community support at www.MommyTimeOut.com and www.facebook.com/MommyTimeOut1, will encourage mothers to start (or continue) to give to themselves so they can be emotionally, physically and mentally able to give to the loves of their lives.

We have also included forms, our exclusive Mommy Time-Out Coupons™ and other Time-Out suggestions to assist the overwhelmed mother in staying organized and more likely to take that Time-Out.

Mommy Time-Out Guidelines™

In order to have a successful Time-Out, think of the guidelines you give your children when you send them to a Time-Out and apply it to yourself:

Play Well With Others Create a support group with friends and/or family that you trust. If they have children, trade babysitting times. If they don't, watch their pets or their house when they go out of town. At the very least, have a reliable babysitter listed among your contacts that you can call when you need that Time-Out.

Justify Your Actions Keep reminding yourself that you have earned this Time-Out. Enjoy every minute - you so deserve it!

Remove Yourself Let your sitter know you cannot be disturbed during this time, unless it is an absolute emergency.

Mommy Time-Out Guidelines™

Set A Timer Set no less than a half hour aside, more if you can, depending on what you plan to do that day. Schedule it at least a day or more ahead of time so you can not only arrange for the sitter, but be both mentally and emotionally prepared for the "me-time" to follow.

Think About Why You're There It's as much for your family as it is for you. Take care of yourself so you have the physical, emotional and mental strength to take care of them.

STAY There! Don't cheat yourself. You have already set a specific amount of time aside for yourself, so stick with it.

Make The Best Of It Block everything and everyone out of your mind except the activity you have planned - and savor every moment!

Mommy Time-Out Guidelines™

You're On Restriction You are not allowed to fold laundry, clean the kitchen, go grocery shopping, go to doctor appointments, or run any errands in general – they do not count as your Mommy Time-Out! NO WORK! Or else it doesn't count and your Time-Out has to start all over again!

Be Consistent Take a Time-Out one to two times a week. They don't all have to be two hours long. A movie on Sunday can easily be followed by a half hour candle lit bubble bath on Wednesday.

Don't Expect Miracles Like anything worthwhile, it's a process. Make it a part of your lifestyle instead of an "extra" thing you do for yourself. The rewards may take time or they may be immediate – but either way, they will happen.

If you follow these guidelines, your Mommy Time-Out will be optimized, which will return you to your family feeling renewed, focused, calm and ready to take on the next challenge. Best of all, you will have more of yourself to give.

Go Out & Play

The kids are with the sitter:

- Playing video games
- Swimming, sledding, etc.
- At the zoo, mall, movies
- On a playdate

Plan ahead:

- Call the sitter, set the time
- Emergency info is on the fridge
- Buy their favorite snacks
- Cash for kids to spend

Nothing beats getting **out of the house** to do something that will help you get **back in touch** with the woman you were before you got lost in hectic schedules and piles of laundry.

Here are some **inexpensive**, **simple** yet **relaxing** things you can do away from home - or at least *outside* of the house.

Mommy Time-Out means Mommy Can

Relax at the park.

sit in one spot for

longer than three

minutes.

Be still...listen...breathe.

Mommy Time-Out

means Mommy Can

get an even pace.

Go running or jogging.

take her

Vitamin D.

Get some sun...remember the sunscreen!

Mommy Time-Out means Mommy Can focus exclusively on her friends.

Meet a friend over a favorite drink.

Mommy Time-Out means Mommy Can

get strength from her friends.

Join a support or prayer group.

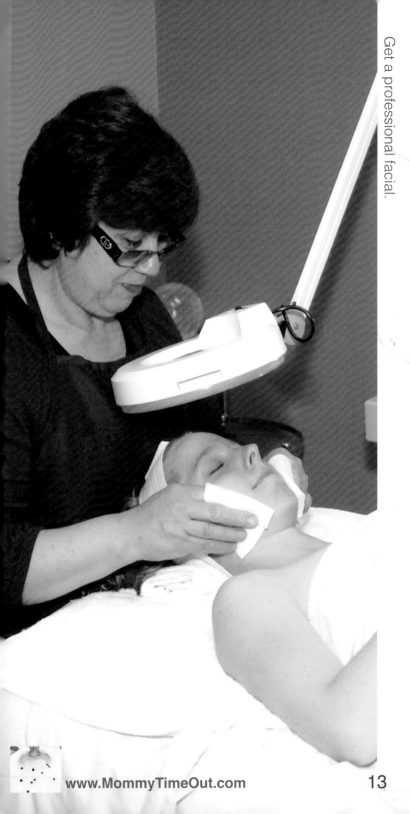

Mommy Time-Out means Mommy Can have a facial not made up of spit, snot, or dirt.

Mommy Time-Out means Mommy Can

eat the whole thing all by herself...

BEFORE it melts.

Treat yourself to your favorite food.

Mommy Time-Out

means Mommy Can

finally have a peaceful

walk.

Mommy Time-Out

means Mommy Can

discover how quiet

the pool can be.

Sit quietly by the pool or lake.

Mommy Time-Out means Mommy Can not only learn Yoga, but DO it.

Practice or learn Yoga.

Have a much needed private conversation with a friend.

Mommy Time-Out means Mommy Can

share her secrets -

without little ears listening.

Mommy Time-Out means Mommy Can do her favorite thing in her favorite spot.

Do something you love in your favorite place

Mommy Time-Out

means

Mommy Can

Get a professional manicure.

Get a professional pedicure.

let someone

else do

the work!

Mommy Time-Out means Mommy Can

Get your hair done professionally.

put every hair in place...

instead of

pulling them all out!

Find a quiet place to write in your journal.

Mommy Time-Out means Mommy Can

sit quietly long enough to form a thought

AND write it down!

Mommy Time-Out means Mommy Can

Have an adult conversation, uninterrupted.

have a real tea party with her friends.

Go window shopping at your own pace.

Mommy Time-Out means Mommy Can

shop until she drops.

Mommy Time-Out means Mommy Can

enjoy that other park -

the one without the swings.

Visit your local botanical or public garden.

Watch a sunrise or sunset.

watch Mother Nature do her thing.

Mommy Time-Outs You Can Do Away From Home

- Art class
- Beach
- Bike ride
- Buy a new outfit
- Class at a junior college
- Coffee - by yourself or with a friend
- Concert
- Cooking class
- Dance class
- Date with spouse
- Facial by a professional
- Gardening
- Girls Night Out
- Go dancing
- Go for a drive
- Gym
- Haircut
- Happy Hour with friends
- Jogging
- Join a group of Bonko
- Lake
- Library
- Lunch/Dinner - by yourself or with a friend
- Make-up done by a professional
- Mall
- Manicure/pedicure
- Massage
- Movies - by yourself or with a friend
- Museum
- Play Bingo
- Play dress up at high-end clothing stores
- Play your favorite sport
- Running
- Serve your community
- Sit and listen to your surroundings
- Sun bathe
- Swimming
- Test drive your favorite sports car
- Visit a state park or landmark
- Walking
- Watch the sunset or sunrise
- Weekend getaway with friends/spouse
- Windowshopping
- Yoga class

Stay In & Relax

The kids are:

- At a birthday party
- Sound asleep
- At playdate/grandparents

Plan ahead:

- Buy supplies when shopping
- Plan the babysitting/playdate
- Get kids tired so they sleep well

With a **little planning ahead**, like buying the bubble bath or nail polish at your next grocery trip, you will have **more time** to relax in your at-home Mommy Time-Out.

Here are a few **simple** yet mind-numbingly **relaxing** things you can do, day or night, to rediscover yourself in the comfort of your own home.

Mommy Time-Out means Mommy Can

read a book with sentences

longer than five words...

and no pop-ups.

Read that book you've been meaning to read.

Mommy Time-Out

means Mommy Can

hear every word.

Reconnect with a friend.

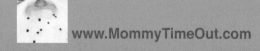

Oh yeah!

Mommy Time-Out means Mommy Can

SLEEP.

Mommy Time-Out means Mommy Can

Write to a friend.

send mail the old-fashioned way.

Mommy Time-Out means Mommy Can

Surf the internet.

have the computer all to herself.

Lose yourself in your favorite TV show or movie.

Mommy Time-Out means Mommy Can

finally control the remote.

Start or update a family scrapbook or photo album.

Mommy Time-Out means Mommy Can save her favorite family memories before she forgets them!

Family Fun Pass

Mommy Time-Out
means Mommy Can
paint five toes in a row
- and let all ten dry -
without interruption.

Give yourself a manicure/pedicure.

www.MommyTimeOut.com

Mommy Time-Out means Mommy Can think about nothing starting right…now.

www.MommyTimeOut.com

45

Mommy Time-Outs You Can Do At Home

- Bake a favorite treat
- Bubble bath
- Creative writing
- Dance to your favorite music
- Date with spouse at home
- Do a puzzle
- Draw/Design
- Exercise DVD
- Facial
- Friend over for a meal
- Game night with friends
- Gardening
- Girls' Night In
- Journal writing
- Knitting
- Learn a new craft
- Listen to your favorite music
- Meditate
- Meet a new neighbor
- Paint a picture
- Paint your nails
- Phone a friend
- Play a video game
- Play an instrument
- Play Glamour Girl with your makeup
- Pottery
- Read a book
- Read the newspaper/comics
- Reminisce over family photos
- Restyle your hair
- Scrapbook
- Sit and do nothing
- Surf the internet
- Take a long shower
- Take a nap
- Take extra time to get ready
- Try out a new recipe
- Update the baby book/family album
- Watch your favorite movie or TV show
- Watch old home movies
- Write a card or letter to a friend
- Yoga

Helpful Forms

To get the most out of this book and the forms that follow, consider using the Mommy Time-Out ideas in this book with the information and community support available at www.MommyTimeOut.com and www.facebook.com/MommyTimeOut1.

These forms are also available for <u>FREE</u> to download from our site, so print out as many as you need, as often as you need them. Share them with your mother friends, show them to your family members - anything to keep the Mommy Time-Out movement going!

Also, while you are there, be sure to subscribe to our <u>FREE</u> weekly Mommy Time-Out email reminder and 'Like' us on Facebook!

See you there!

<u>To Make My Mommy Time-Out Happen</u>
Sample

For my Mommy Time-Out I will <u>get a mani/pedi, then lunch with Feli</u> on (Day): <u>Thursday, August 2</u> from (Time): <u>11:30a.m.</u> to <u>2 p.m.</u>.

My child(ren) will <u>go to the park then lunch at home</u> with <u>Sofia and Katie.</u>

The caregiver is <u>Oma</u>, whom I _____have __X__have not called to ask him/her to sit with my child(ren). If I have not called the caregiver yet, I will do so no later than <u>Monday, July 30</u>.

For my Mommy Time-Out I will need:	For my Mommy Time-Out my child(ren) will need:
<u>Money</u> <u>Open-Toed Shoes/Sandals</u> <u>Gas in the car</u>	<u>Snacks for the park</u> <u>Sippy cups for the park</u> <u>Their favorite lunch food</u>

which I can get when I <u>go grocery shopping on Monday</u>.

To Make My Mommy Time-Out Happen

For my Mommy Time-Out I will _____ on

(Day):_____ from (Time): _____ to _____.

My child(ren) will_____ with _____.

The caregiver is _____, whom I ____have ____have not called

him/her/them to ask them to sit with my child(ren). If I have not called the

caregiver yet, I will do so no later than _____.

For my Mommy Time-Out I will
need:

_____
_____
_____
_____
_____

For my Mommy Time-Out
my child(ren) will need:

_____
_____
_____
_____
_____

which I can get when I _____.

Babysitter/Caregiver List

Babysitter/Caregiver	Phone Numbers(s)	Available to watch
Oma	*555-1234*	*Wednesday-Friday day Saturday & Sunday nights*

Download more copies FREE at www.MommyTimeOut.com!

Calendar

Sunday	Monday	Tuesday	Wednesday	Thursday	Friday	Saturday

Download more copies FREE at www.MommyTimeOut.com!

Emergency Contact Information

Child's Name_____ D.O.B._____ Sex: M F

FIRST PARENT

_____ (____)_____ (____)_____ (____)_____
Parent's/Guardian's Name   Cell Phone   Work Phone   Home Phone

_____
Address   City   ST   Zip

SECOND PARENT

_____ (____)_____ (____)_____ (____)_____
Parent's/Guardian's Name   Cell Phone   Work Phone   Home Phone

_____
Address   City   ST   Zip

ALTERNATE CONTACT

This person will be contacted in case of emergency if neither parent above can be reached.

_____ (____)_____ (____)_____ (____)_____
Parent's/Guardian's Name   Cell Phone   Work Phone   Home Phone

_____
Address   City   ST   Zip

Download more copies FREE at www.MommyTimeOut.com!

Medical Information and Release Form

PEDIATRICIAN

_____   (_____)_____
Pediatrician's Name   Phone Number

_____
Closest/Preferred Hospital   Address

INSURANCE

_____   _____
Insurance Company   Policy Number

ALLERGIES/SPECIAL HEALTH CONDITIONS

_____
_____
_____
_____

I authorize all medical and surgical treatment, X-ray, laboratory, anesthesia, and other medical and/or hospital procedures as may be performed or prescribed by the attending physician and/or paramedics for my child and waive my right to informed consent of treatment. This waiver applies only in the event that neither parent/guardian can be reached in the case of an emergency.

_____   _____
Parent's/Guardian's Signature   Date

MOMMY TIME-OUT COUPON

This coupon is presented to (Mom's Name) _____ to take a

(length of time)_____ Mommy Time-Out on (Date)_____.

With Love and Gratitude,

_____
Signature

MOMMY TIME-OUT COUPON

This coupon is presented to (Mom's Name) _____ to take a

(length of time)_____ Mommy Time-Out on (Date)_____.

With Love and Gratitude,

_____
Signature

Suggestion: Include movie tickets, money, gift cards, etc. to add to her Mommy Time-Out experience!

Download more copies FREE at www.MommyTimeOut.com!

MOMMY TIME-OUT COUPON

This coupon is presented to (Mom's Name) _____ to take a

(length of time)_____ Mommy Time-Out on (Date)_____.

With Love and Gratitude,

_____
Signature

= =

MOMMY TIME-OUT COUPON

This coupon is presented to (Mom's Name) _____ to take a

(length of time)_____ Mommy Time-Out on (Date)_____.

With Love and Gratitude,

_____
Signature

Suggestion: Include movie tickets, money, gift cards, etc. to add to her Mommy Time-Out experience!

Download more copies FREE at www.MommyTimeOut.com!

On My Mommy Time-Out I Want To...

1. Go Skydiving

2. Try new restaurant that just opened

3. Call Feli and catch up

4. Finish script

5. _____

6. _____

7. _____

8. _____

9. _____

10. _____

Write down some specific things you've been wanting to do so that when you are taking your Mommy Time-Out, whether unexpected or planned, you will have plenty of ideas!

Download more copies FREE at www.MommyTimeOut.com!

Afterword

I was inspired to create this Mommy Time-Out book after watching an episode on Oprah in 2008 in which an overwhelmed mother had accidentally left her child in the car, with fatal results (www.oprah.com/relationships/An-Overwhelmed-Mothers-Deadly-Mistake/1).

My heart went out to this mother - and all mothers - that have experienced this type of trauma in their lives. And I felt that could so easily be me on any given day. Then I wondered how many more women feel that way and struggle to take time for themselves, or maybe never do. And so the inspiration was born.

I called my sister-in-law Kelley, a talented photographer who agreed to shoot the photos. Then I called my friend Colleen and asked her, if I got the pictures done for the book, would she help me write it? She did and now, four years later, this little book has evolved from a print only book, to a blog site, and eventually a phone app. More than any of that, it has become a movement that we hope each of you will help build and share in.

Feli Robles
Palm Springs, CA
August 2012

Special Thanks

The creators of this book would like to give a heartfelt thank you to all the mothers and supporters of this book that took time out of their busy schedules and believed in us, including:

Lourdes Boyer
Sharon Brubaker
Sandra Castro
Nadine Crowder
Holly Dang (Nail Pro, Palm Springs, CA)
Shelly Dunlap
Karen Ephrian
Marie Gaddy
Lola Granillo (Lola's Signature Touch,
    Palm Desert, CA)
Goya Gutierrez-Luna
Diana Hernandez
Sandra Hernandez
Vivian Hernandez
April Herrera
Leigh Lopez
Jeannette McCarroll

Angel McClinton
Heather Mekemson
Arcelia Mendiola
Meredith Milder
Jasmine Pinson
Leah Pinson
Jeannette Pryor
Marcus Pryor
MJ Saltz
Veronica Sanchez
Katie Scott (Baby Face Spa, Austin, TX)
Ronda Sommaripa
Nora Thomas
Dawn Tiszai
Aracely Urrutia
Arlette Vasquez

We would especially like to thank Mony Patel, our business partner and investor, who saw our vision and believed in us enough to take us one big step closer to realizing our dreams. Thank you, Mony!

Without all of you, this book would not be what it is or where it is: a tool in the hands of mothers who need balance in their lives. We love you and thank you from the bottom of our hearts.

Acknowledgments

Feli Robles: I would like to thank God for putting this burning desire in my heart to create a book that would help overwhelmed mothers remember to always put themselves on their "To Do List". To my two most precious gifts, Sofia (8) and Katie (6), you make motherhood worth it, I love you both so very much. To their father, Matthew Robles, thank you for being supportive while this book was being created. My mother, Andrea Hernandez, you are a true warrior and amazing mother, thank you for believing in me and encouraging me to follow my dreams. To my dear friend Grace Armenta, from the moment I brought this book idea to you, you encouraged me the whole way; thank you for your love and support, my heart is forever grateful to you. Last, but certainly not least, thank you Jay Shanker. You've been a long time friend and trusted legal counselor who often did pro-bono work on my behalf simply because you believed in me. Thank you for all your legal advice – and friendship - throughout the years.

Colleen Phillips: To the love of my life, my best friend, my sounding board my most trusted editor and our girls' favorite babysitter, my husband Kevin Phillips, thanks for covering for me so I can have my Time-Outs, I love you. To Casey (5), Keira (3) and Cali (2 months), my inspiration to be the best mommy I can be. I miss you when I am on Time-Out but I am glad I did it, for all our sakes!! I love each of you with all of my heart and then some. Finally, to my mother, Wally "Oma" Dina, for all the times you entertained the girls while I worked on this book, and your support and encouragement over the years to follow my dreams wherever they took me - thank you, I love you!

Kelley Hernandez: I would like to thank God for blessing me with my husband Abraham and two beautiful children Isabella (13) and Drew (9). I have learned and continue to learn so much about myself and life through them. In times of celebration or sadness I have them to laugh and cry with. I am so grateful to have such a supportive husband who even through the REALLY tough times is still willing to stick it out with me. Thank you, honey, for working so hard so that I could stay home for as long as I did. Isabella thank you for being the daughter I always wanted. I love that you call me higher as a person and a mother. Drew, you have taught me true unconditional love. Thank you for all the snuggle time. Last, but not least, to all the moms who have guided me through this adventure. You know who you are. I couldn't have done it without you. Thank you!

Join Us!

Thank you for purchasing our book and joining us in getting the word out that Mommy Time-Outs will no longer be the exception to the rule, but <u>the rule itself</u> in the lives of mothers everywhere.

In addition to this book, the tools on our website, and our ever-growing online community, our upcoming projects include the Mommy Time-Out Cookbook™ and the Mommy Time-Out Phone App™, that we hope to have released in 2014.

Be the first to know of these and many more exciting tools, gifts and events by subscribing to our FREE weekly MTO Newsletter at <u>www.MommyTimeOut.com</u>.

Together let's keep the Mommy Time-Out Movement growing!